Destroy the Enemy in Hand-to-Hand Combat

Maj. Gen. A. A. Tarasov

Trans., Boris Karpa

ISBN: 1489533281
ISBN-13: 978-1489533289

DEDICATION

This translated edition is dedicated to Mechthild Czapp.

CONTENTS

ACKNOWLEDGEMENTS

I would like to thank Konstantin Vikhornov of the «Polyn» search team for making available the original Russian text online, and for their work putting to rest the fallen Soviet soldiers of World War II.

I would also like to thank my editor Yuri Mataev for his invaluable help.

FOREWORD

Russian military culture has always valued and rated highly the ability of the individual soldier in close combat. Already in the 18th century, Alexander Suvorov, the fabled Russian general, taught his men to supplement marksmanship with hand-to-hand combat skills: "Shoot rarely, but accurately, stab fiercely with the bayonet. The bullet is a fool, the bayonet is a winner!"

This emphasis on hand-to-hand combat has remained with the Russian military through the centuries. In the 19th century, Platov's Cossacks were renowned for their skill with the shashka - a wickedly-curved cavalry sabre, optimized not for hit-and-run thrusting attacks, like the straight sabres of Western European troops, but for vicious close-combat battles. The shashka rewarded the skill-at-arms and tenacity of those who dared to engage in a melee and not back down.

Soviet Communism, which destroyed many noble Russian traditions, did not destroy the Russian tradition of close combat. Not only members of the military, but law enforcement and even high school students of both genders were encouraged to learn how to fight with bayonets, entrenching tools, and even improvised weapons, like full-sized shovels. Bayonet-fighting became a competitive sport that is practiced in Russia to this day.

This was done not only for the direct practical benefits of close-combat skills, but to prepare the young men and women of Russia for combat spiritually and mentally. It was thought that troops who were psychologically prepared to stab their fellow man with a bayonet or lop his head off with a shovel would be tenacious and brave fighters in other aspects of combat.

Hence it should be clear why, when the Nazis invaded the Soviet Union in June of 1941, despite the advantages that the armies of the Reich held in technology, firepower, and surprise, they were still astonished by the tenacity of Russian soldiers, and their skill in close combat. Almost every branch of the Soviet armed forces trained in bayonet combat--even the navy. Indeed, there are recorded incidents where submarine crews--certainly unlikely to ever use that skill--asked to be trained in bayonet combat on their own time.

The bayonet-charges of Russian troops, their skilled use of their infantry shovels and the stocks of their rifles is the stuff of legends. What you hold in your hands now is part of that legend--one of the manuals which the very men who fought in the basements of Stalingrad and in the streets of Berlin used.

But it is not merely a piece of history. While it is likely that any American who shoots regularly is a better shot than the average Soviet conscript, many shooters are entirely unprepared to use their shotgun or rifle in close combat. Given that most self-defense encounters occur at a range of under twenty feet (Soviet tacticians considered everything under one hundred feet to be 'close combat'), neglecting one's close combat skill might become a fatal mistake. For those with an interest in combat and tactics, this book contains tips on cross-terrain movement and obstacle crossing.

While no man can learn martial arts or survival skills simply by reading a book, familiarizing yourself with the tactics and skills of the men who fought in some of the toughest battles of human history--and emerged victorious--is always a good start.

The book is recommended for those interested in military history, self-defense, or emergency preparedness.

-- Boris Karpa, translator

Publisher's Note: The quality of the drawings in Destroy the Enemy in Hand-to-Hand Combat is not due to any error on our part or the part of our printer. They appear exactly as they appeared in the Russian original.

Destroy the Enemy in Hand-to-Hand Combat

Major-General

A. A. TARASOV

Move swiftly and stealthily,

Throw the grenade far and accurately,

Strike with your bayonet and stock confidently!

USSR PEOPLE'S COMISSARIAT FOR DEFENSE MILITARY PRESS

MOSCOW, 1941

Hitler's brigands wish to capture our land, our bread, and our oil. They want to restore in our country the rule of the Czar and the landlords, to Germanize the free peoples of the Soviet Union, and turn them into the slaves of German princes and barons. Never shall this come to pass! Death to the Fascist vermin!

The enemy cannot bear the Red Army's bayonet blows. Strike the Fascist vermin with the bullet, with the grenade, with the bayonet!

FIGHTER!

The deadly and cunning foe of Your Motherland – German fascism – is armed to the teeth with weapons and technical implements of warfare.

That said, the German fascist hordes avoid meeting us in hand-to-hand skirmishes, for our fighters have shown that they have never had, and do not have now, equals in courage and agility in hand-to-hand battle.

We must, however, contend with the enemy's technology and tactics. You must master perfectly the art of approaching the enemy, the art of closing with him on the battlefield.

You must learn to move in such a way that enemy fire, no matter how strong, is unable to hinder our maneuvers, our advance and our assault.

Therefore, when battling our vicious foe:

- Move swiftly and stealthily!
- Throw your grenade far and accurately!
- Strike with your bayonet and stock surely!

LEARN TO MOVE SWIFTLY AND SKILLFULLY ACROSS THE FIELD OF BATTLE!

To close rapidly with the opponent and destroy him with the grenade and bayonet, to reduce losses from the opponent's fire, every fighter must be able to move in a manner that is both technically and tactically correct, as well as cross any artificial or natural obstacle with speed and skill.

Learning and training in the methods of battlefield movement and obstacle crossing are among the most important elements of physical training for combat.

Skillful and tactically correct movement is the most important means of concealing one's approach from the opponent and ensuring a surprise attack for the purpose of destroying the opponent in hand-to-hand combat.

The fastest kind of movement on the battlefield is that which minimizes the effect of enemy fire.

Remember that the opponent watches your movements, and therefore you, too, must watch him constantly and vigilantly.

In circumstances where ahead of you lies cover that conceals a man standing tall, in dead spaces where the opponent's bullets do not reach, move at a brisk pace or at a run, without stopping.

As the cover gets lower, begin moving in a crouch.

Fig. 1: Moving in a crouch

For this purpose, crouch by bending your knees, tilt your torso forward without bending your back, look forward and walk forward calmly and without tensing (Fig. 1). To accelerate either take wider steps or start running. Crouch based on the height of the cover – the lower the cover, the lower you should crouch. If the cover is low enough that you can no longer move forward in a crouch, move to a prone position or switch to brief sprints.

Learn the technique of the sprint

To jump up rapidly from a prone position, place both your hands at chest level, with the left hand placed palm down, while the right hand, holding the rifle, is placed palm up. Push with both hands against the ground, while simultaneously pulling one leg forward. Push sharply with the bent leg while tilting your torso forward, run rapidly to your goal and immediately drop to the prone shooting position. (Fig. 2)

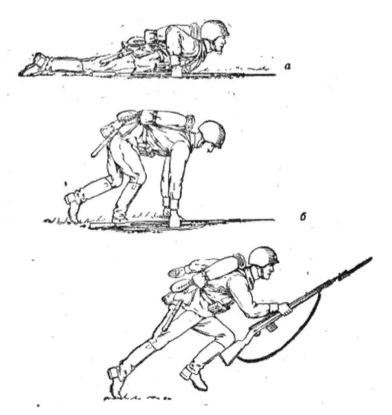

Fig. 2 Leaping up and commencing a sprint – a) raising the hands and rifle to the chest
b) pushing off against the ground and pulling a leg up
c) rushing forward for the sprint

As you reach the last step of your sprint, throw your right foot forward and slightly to the right, simultaneously placing your left hand with the palm on the ground, its fingers near the right foot, and, supporting your weight first on the left hand, and then on the left hip, lie down on your left side (Fig 3.) After this, immediately lie down on your belly, while simultaneously shifting your rifle forward for reloading or firing.

Crawl aside after the sprint, leaning on your forearms and the tips of your feet, lifting your torso slightly to avoid catching on the ground with your equipment (Fig. 4)

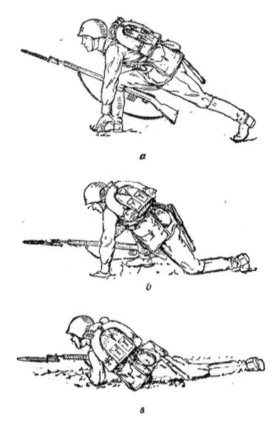

Fig 3. Moving to the prone position after a sprint

a) Move your leg forward and bend down towards the knee while lowering your hand for support

b) and c) getting down while supporting yourself on the elbow and hip to go prone

Fig 4. Crawling aside on your forearms and toes/tips of your feet

Learn and train in crawling

The simplest and fastest way to crawl is crawling on half-fours. (Fig. 5). Use this method where useful concealment or cover is available (high grass, low bushes, ditches, etc.)

From a run or from a prone position get on your left or right knee, pull it up as much as possible under your belly, and, moving on your knees and forearms (or even palms, depending on the height of your cover) move forward. Hold your rifle by its sling, with the bolt facing upward. Grasp it as tightly as possible with your right hand, pressing your thumb to the foregrip of the rifle.

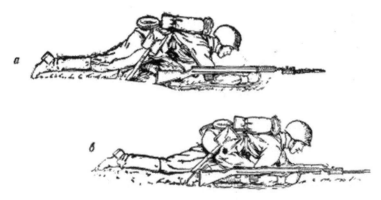

Fig. 5: Crawling on half-fours

a) Moving the right hand and left leg forward

b) Moving the left hand and right leg forward

As cover gets lower, or across open terrain, one should crawl flat against the ground *(Fig. 6)*.

As you lie down low against the ground, bend your left (right) leg at the knee and pull it up as much as possible, while extending the opposing arm to its full length. Pulling yourself up on the arm and pushing with the inner side of the bent leg, move forward, while simultaneously bending and extending the other arm and leg, respectively. Do not lift your torso while moving. Do not stand on your foot or knee. Keep your legs mostly relaxed when pulling yourself up, pull in the foot of the bent leg, while relaxing and extending the foot of the other leg and pulling yourself up.

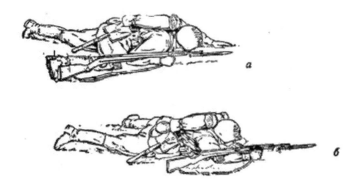

Fig. 6. Low-crawling:

a) Moving the right hand and left leg forward

b) Moving the left hand and right leg forward

When crawling across puddles, mud, or sand, hold your rifle as portrayed in Fig. 7, while taking alternate steps with the elbows.

Fig. 7 Low-crawling on the elbows

TO MOVE RAPIDLY AND STEALTHILY ACROSS THE BATTLEFIELD, TRAIN IN OBSTACLE-CROSSING DAILY AND IN VARIOUS CONDITIONS

Learn to cross deep obstacles (ditches, creeks, ravines) using a log.

1st method: Sit astride the log, put your two hands in front of you, and, placing your weight on your hands, yank your legs backwards, rise on your hands and move to sit closer to your hands (Fig. 8). Move on, repeating those movements.

Fig. 8: Moving seated on a log

a) Initial position b) Position after having moved one's hands forward and moved the body towards the hands with a simultaneous backwards leg motion

2nd method: stand on a log, bend your legs at the knees slightly and move forward bravely, with short, rapid steps (Fig. 9). Use your arms to help yourself keep balance but do not move them widely or too rapidly. Do not look down, but forward in front of you. When crossing deep and dangerous obstacles, make a 'railing' from rope (Fig. 10.)

7

Fig. 9. Moving across a log standing.

Fig. 10 Moving across a log standing, holding a rope.

Cross small obstacles by jumping and landing on one leg. Push off with the stronger leg at a run. Land on the other leg after leaping over the obstacle and immediately resume moving forward (Fig. 11 and 12).

Fig. 11 Jumping to land on one foot across a horizontal obstacle

Fig. 12 Jumping to land on one foot across a vertical obstacle

Cross broader obstacles by jumping and landing on both legs, as shown in Fig 13. Mountain creeks and swamps with plentiful tussocks can be crossed by stepping or leaping on the rocks or tussocks (Fig. 14.). Do not hurry, and take your time to choose the nearest or most stable rocks and hardiest tussocks to rest your foot on. Do not stand for too long on one foot. Use your arms to help keep balance and lengthen your jump distance.

Fig. 13: Positions of the body while leaping across a ditch or ravine to land on both legs.4

Fig. 14. Crossing a mountain river by leaping from rock to rock

Fig. 15 A 'stepping jump' at the moment when one foot rests on the obstacle, and the other is being carried over.

Cross low obstacles — palisades, broken trees, rocks, walls, pipes — with a jump in which the foot steps on the obstacle (Fig. 15). During the step, bend your leg at the knee, and then, without straightening the knee or raising your torso, carry the other foot across the obstacle, use it to step on the ground on the other side, and move on rapidly and without delay.

Cross taller obstacles with a jump, stepping on the obstacle with a foot while simultaneously resting your left hand on it (Fig. 16).

Fig. 16: A side-jump while resting one's hand, at the moment of finding purchase and beginning to carry the free leg over.

Push off with the left leg at a run, place your right leg on the obstacle simultaneously with the left hand, move your torso rapidly forward and immediately carry the left leg under the right one, place it on the other side of the obstacle, and move on swiftly.

Cross low fences and one-row wire obstacles with a jump, resting your left hand on the obstacle.

Running up to the obstacle from the side, at an angle of about 40-45 degrees, rest your left hand on the obstacle, push off with the right leg and rapidly carry first the outstretched left leg, and immediately afterwards, the right leg, across the obstacle (Fig. 17-18).

Fig. 17. A sideways jump with one hand for support —

positions of the body during the jump.

Fig. 18. A sideways jump with one hand for support -

the position of the body at the moment of using one's hand

for support to carry the legs across the fence.

Cross high obstacles by first propping yourself up on two hands, and then proceed as in Fig. 19, or rest your right hand on the opposite side of the obstacle and carry the legs across (Fig. 20).

Fig. 19: Jumping based on two hands - positions of the body during the jump.

Climbing across obstacles taller than your arms extended upwards.

First method: After a brisk run, push off with the stronger leg about a meter away from the obstacle, while simultaneously throwing the other foot forward so the front of the foot hits the obstacle, and, using the torso's forward and upward movement, grab onto to the upper edge of the obstacle; then, pushing off with the foot resting against the obstacle and simultaneously pulling yourself up with your hands, move on to rest on both hands and roll across the obstacle as seen in Fig. 20.

Second method: With a "hold": move up to the obstacle, jump, grab the upper edge with your hands, turn your left side towards it, and, stepping with your feet on the obstacle or a single powerful swing, grab on to the upper edge with the heel of your right foot and roll across in the manner most comfortable to you (Fig. 21).

(See figures on next page.)

*Fig. 20: one of the methods for crossing a tall fence,
at the moment of shifting both legs off to one side.*

Fig. 21: Crossing an obstacle (fence or wall) with a «catch»

If you cannot cross the obstacle independently, use the aid of a comrade and help him in turn (Fig. 22-25).

Fig. 22: Climbing a fence or wall
with the help of one fighter

Fig. 23: Helping the last fighter
climb the obstacle

u

Fig. 24: Climbing an
obstacle with the aid of
two fighters:

a) Fighters with sticks
(large shovels, etc.)

b) Helping a fighter climb
a tall obstacle

б

Fig. 25: Using a rope to climb an obstacle

Learn to jump into and leap out of a trench (Fig. 26-30).

Land softly, on the tiptoes, and sit down, so your legs absorb the impact like springs. Always try to land facing towards the nearest enemy. As you land, hold the rifle to be ready to shoot or stab.

Use these methods of moving and overcoming obstacles, and train to do them while throwing grenades, shooting, and practicing bayonet combat, on any terrain, during the day or at night, and in any weather.

Train your agility, stamina, and skill for action in an assault.

A tenacious, agile and confident fighter acts decisively and bravely. One such fighter is worth ten men.

Fig. 26-27: Jumping down into a ravine from a sitting position or from a prone position.

Fig. 29: Jumping down from a tall obstacle by hanging on one's hands.

Fig. 29. Jumping down into a trench or communications passage by resting on its edge.

Fig. 30: Jumping out of a trench or communications ditch:
a) Rest your hands on the edge of the breastwork
b) The moment of resting the hands and right knee on the berm
c) Moving the right leg forward after resting the left leg on the breastwork
d)Running forward

TRAIN IN THROWING GRENADES FROM ANY POSITION WITH SPEED AND ACCURACY

When attacking the enemy, at a range of 35-45 meters use accurate grenade throws to force him to cease fire; when closing with the opponent, exterminate the survivors with bullet, bayonet, and stock.

Follow these rules when throwing grenades on the move, during an assault.

Running up to the range at which you can reliably throw grenades, take a step forward with the right foot, simultaneously leaning on it and turning your torso to the right, rapidly raise the right hand upwards and back, and then, straightening your right leg while moving the left one forward, rapidly throw the grenade from behind your back, across the right shoulder — forward at an angle of 40-43 degrees. Yank your left arm backwards to increase the speed of the throw. Let go of the grenade as it passes over your right shoulder. As you throw the grenade, pass your right arm over the shoulder, elbow forward. During the throw, shift the weight of the body rapidly to your left leg (Fig. 31).

(See figure on next page.)

Fig 31. Throwing the grenade
overarm in movement.

a) Step with the right leg and begin
the throw.

b) Step with the left leg and continue
the throw.

c) Position just before letting go of
the grenade.

Exterminate attacking opponents by throwing grenades from the trench (as seen in Fig. 32), from behind various forms of cover, and from a prone position.

To improve the range and accuracy of your grenade throw from a prone position, rest the rifle to your right and prepare the grenade for throwing. Turn to your left side, and, immediately pulling up your legs and resting the palm of the left hand near the left knee, move your torso as far back and to the right as you can manage; push off with your left hand, and, straightening your leg, raise yourself while bending at the waist, and immediately throw the grenade forward (Fig. 33). After the throw, drop to the ground immediately, turning both palms towards the ground, and either lie down to a shooting position or grab your rifle, leap up and rush the enemy — exterminate them with bullet, bayonet, or stock.

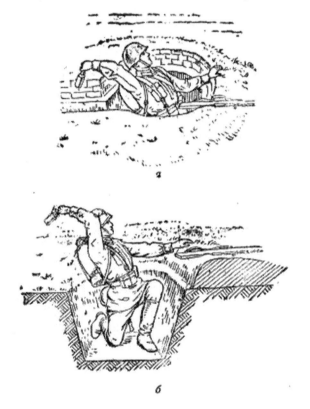

Fig. 32 Throwing the grenade across the shoulder from a trench cell:

a) Approximate pose when throwing from a standing position

b) Approximate pose when throwing from a kneeling position

When throwing from behind tall cover (trees, house corners, etc.), throw grenades or grenade packs with a straight arm from the side (Fig. 34).

Move the right leg backward and rest your weight on it, move the right arm back, straight, while simultaneously turning your torso to the right and back (as if coiling it), and then swing. After the swing, simultaneously turning your torso and arm upward and forward, throw the grenade or grenade pack at the opponent.

(See figure on next two pages.)

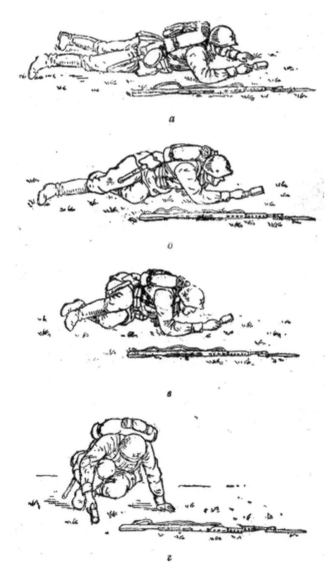

Fig. 33: Throwing the grenade from a prone position across the shoulder:

a) Resting prone before the throw

b) Pulling up the left leg and arm

c) Pulling up the right leg

d) The beginning of the swing,

(Opposite)

e) Continuation of the swing,
f) Beginning of the throw,
g) Position after the throw

Learn to let go of the grenade on time. A belated release could cause the grenade to fly left, and an early release — to the right, which could cause you not only to miss the enemy, but to injure the man next to you.

Remember the admonishments of Marshal of the Soviet Union Comrade Voroshilov - the grenade is a form of powerful pocket artillery. Train tenaciously in the skills and tactics of combat grenade use.

Fig 34. Throwing the grenade with a straight arm from the side
a) The swing, b) The approximate position after having released the grenade while throwing from behind a tree

LEARN TO USE THE BAYONET IN HAND-TO-HAND COMBAT THE SUVOROV WAY

Move bravely and rapidly towards the nearest enemy, strike him down with your bullet — or, when it is not possible to shoot, destroy him with the bayonet. For this purpose, keep running, and then place the rifle over your leg in the ready position (Fig. 35): Push the rifle forward with the right hand, with the bayonet at neck height and in line with the left eye, while simultaneously grabbing it with the left hand over the right, and with the right — by the grip of the stock.

Fig. 35: The ready position for combat on the move

The right hand should be kept level with your groin, slightly in front of it. Do not tense your arms, so as to be ready for rapid movement with your rifle. Do not brace the stock of your rifle against your right forearm. Look at your opponent, follow his every move. Deflect his weapon if he attempts to stab first, and immediately stab him or strike him with the stock.

Based on the situation, stab: only with your hands, with no lunge (short thrust), with a lunge onto either leg (normally the left one) without shifting your left hand (medium thrust) or while shifting your rifle in your left hand (long thrust). During the thrust move the rifle forward rapidly, with strength, slightly faster than the lunging leg! Move the leg forward in the lunge along the shortest path possible, do not raise it high, and plant it heel first. Use the other leg to propel your lunging leg and torso, straighten it out completely, turning the foot to point sideways (Fig. 36-40).

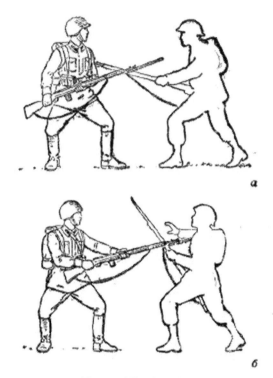

Fig. 36: The short thrust
a) During the swing b) During the thrust

Fig. 37: The medium thrust. Shown during
a thrust with a lunge.

Fig. 38: The long thrust: shown during
a thrust with a lunge.

Train to stab in every direction.

Turn right, left, and backwards on your left heel, finishing the turn to face in the correct direction. With the turn complete, place your right leg a short step's distance behind the left. During a turn, keep your rifle at the ready, only lifting it to your left shoulder, with the bayonet facing you. After you are finished turning, immediately return the rifle to the ready position.

Fig 39: The long thrust — engaging
an entrenched opponent by stabbing downwards from the breastwork.

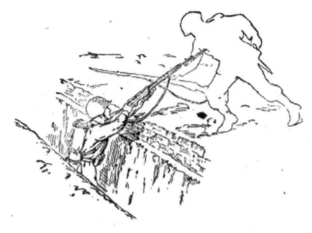

Fig. 40: The long thrust — engaging an opponent on a breastwork by stabbing upwards from the trench.

Learn to spin right on both heels, as shown in Fig. 41. After the turn, thrust immediately with a lunge onto the left leg, or move forward.

During a bayonet fight, move forward, to the sides, or back, by pushing off with the toe of the front or rear foot and simultaneously stepping in the required direction with your other foot; then, pull up the pushing foot the length of the step.

Fig. 41: Posture after turning right and backwards.   *Fig. 42: Deflecting the opponent's weapon to the right.*

Deliver thrusts and blows with the buttstock directly to the undefended parts of the opponent's body. If he protects himself, first deflect his weapon or use deception.

Deceive thus: threaten to thrust from the left or right of his rifle, and when he is moving to deflect your thrust, shift the bayonet to the other side and thrust forward. If he holds his bayonet low, move the bayonet across his rifle. This can also be done by first pushing down the opponent's rifle — thrust at the moment that he begins resisting your push.

An experienced foe will attempt to attack first — train, and be always ready, to deflect his weapon and immediately engage him with your bayonet or stock. Deflect thrusts to the chest to the right or left.

Fig. 43: Deflecting the opponent's weapon to the left.

When deflecting, do not make wide swings with the rifle, to avoid giving your opponent time to shift his bayonet and stab you.

To deflect to the right: (Fig. 42) Yanking the left hand forward and to the right, while simultaneously turning the rifle with its bolt leftwards, strike forcefully with your rifle's front grip on the opponent's weapon and immediately stab him or slash his right hand with a bladed bayonet.

To deflect to the left: (Fig. 43) Yanking the left hand to the left and slightly forward, while simultaneously turning the rifle with its bolt rightwards, strike forcefully with your rifle's front grip on the opponent's weapon and immediately stab him or slash his left hand with a bladed bayonet, or deliver a blow with your buttstock from the side. (Fig. 46-47).

Deflect thrusts directed to your stomach or lower, downwards and to the right (Fig. 44). For this purpose, pull your left hand back rapidly, sending the bayonet in a counter-clockwise motion that ends with it pointing downwards and to the right, striking the opponent's weapon with your rifle's foregrip. Follow up with an immediate thrust. During the deflection, turn your rifle's bolt to the left, and lower the right elbow.

Fig. 44: Deflecting downward and to the right.

Fig. 45: Deflecting downward and to the left.

Deflect the thrust of an opponent who attacks from the left with a downward blow (Fig. 45). For this purpose, turn rapidly left on your left leg, moving your rifle so the bayonet faces down and striking the opponent's rifle. Immediately, in the same motion, with a step or lunge onto the right leg, **strike the enemy in the face with the butt of your rifle stock.** (Fig 46).

Fig. 46: A forward blow with the buttstock.

A roundhouse blow with a buttstock (Fig. 47) is to be used after deflecting the opponent's rifle to the left. For this purpose, step forward rapidly with the left leg, turn on the toes of the left foot and, moving the right leg forward, deliver a rapid blow with the sharp corner of your buttstock to your opponent's head. The faster you turn your torso to the left and straighten your right leg, the stronger the blow will be.

Fig. 47:A roundhouse blow with the buttstock

Should the opponent evade the roundhouse blow, catch up to him with a forward blow with the rear of the buttstock, or a bayonet thrust. Evade or block the opponent's blows, as seen in Fig. 48-49.

Fig. 48: Blocking a roundhouse blow with a buttstock   *Fig. 49: Blocking a downward blow with the buttstock*

At close range, after a deflection, strike the opponent with the foregrip of your rifle or a bladed bayonet on his head or neck. After a leftward deflection strike to the right, and vice versa. When delivering blows with the bladed bayonet, pull the rifle back rapidly in order to slash your opponent (Fig. 50-51).

Fig. 50: Striking with the foregrip from the left.

Fig. 51: Striking with the foregrip from the right.

An experienced fighter can defeat the enemy in hand-to-hand combat using not only a rifle with a bayonet, but one without a bayonet, or even a shovel.

The ready position for a rifle without a bayonet or a large shovel is shown in Fig. 52-53.

During an attack, deflect thrusts in the same way as you would with a rifle equipped with a bayonet, and respond immediately with thrusts or blows to the head (Fig. 54-55.)

In the hands of an experienced fighter, the small infantry shovel also becomes an awe-inspiring weapon. Learn to fight with the small shovel.

Carry out all deflections and blows with the shovel rapidly, sharply and fluidly. Simultaneously with grabbing the opponent's rifle with the left hand close the distance rapidly and deliver blows with the shovel to his head from the right or left side (Fig. 56-62).

Fig. 52: The ready position for a rifle without a bayonet.

Fig. 53: The ready position for a large shovel.

Fig 54: Thrusting at the opponent's neck with a shovel's blade

Fig. 55: Striking the opponent's neck from the left with the large shovel

Fig 56: *Ready position with the small infantry shovel. a) from the front, b) from the side.*

Fig. 57: *Deflecting downwards and to the right with an infantry shovel.*

Fig. 58. *A blow from the right — grabbing the opponent's rifle after a deflection downwards and to the right, and swinging for the blow.*

Fig. 59: Deflecting to the left with the light infantry shovel

*Fig. 58. A blow from the left — grabbing the opponent's rifle after a
deflection downwards and to the left, and swinging for the blow*

Fig. 61: Deflecting to the right with a light infantry shovel

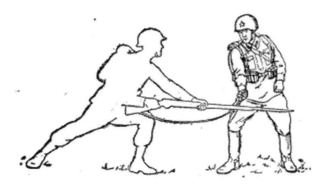

Fig. 62: Deflecting downwards and to the left with a light infantry shovel, followed by a turn to the left.

LEARN TO DISARM THE ENEMY

If the opponent menaces you with a revolver at close range, step left and forward with the left leg, simultaneously rapidly shifting your torso left. With your left hand, grab the opponent by his hand while deflecting the opponent's right arm away from you. Immediately afterward, grab the revolver's barrel with your right hand, and yank on it so as to try and break the opponent's index finger, while simultaneously kicking him (Fig. 63).

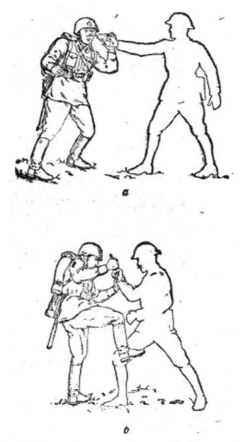

Fig. 63: Disarming an attacker armed with a revolver

a) Deflecting the revolver rightward with the left hand-to-hand b) Capturing the opponent's weapon hand and ripping away the revolver while delivering a toe-kick to the groin.

Fig. 64: Disarming an attacker with a rifle:
Deflecting the opponent's rifle rightward with the right arm.

Fig. 65: Disarming an attacker with a rifle
a) Grabbing the opponent's rifle after deflecting it rightward with the right arm.
b) Headbutting the opponent in the face (with helmet or without).

Fig. 66: Disarming an attacker with a rifle:
Deflecting the opponent's rifle leftward with the left arm.

Fig. 67: Disarming an attacker with a rifle:
a) Grabbing the opponent's rifle after deflecting it leftward with your left arm.
b) Kicking the opponent in the groin.

To disarm an opponent attacking you with a rifle, deflect his weapon with your forearm (Fig. 64). Grabbing the rifle with both hands, yank it towards you, while simultaneously kicking the opponent's legs or genitals, or headbutt him in the face with your helmet (Fig. 65).

When deflecting to the left, grab the rifle with your right hand under the opponent's left hand, and act as shown on Fig. 66-67, attempting to rip the opponent's left hand off the rifle and yank it away, while simultaneously kicking at the opponent's groin.

ABOUT THE TRANSLATOR

Boris Karpa is a writer and translator. He is currently working on a Ph.D. in History at the University of Tel Aviv. If you have any questions or comments, regarding this book or other issues, you may write to him at microbalrog@gmail.com

33785973R00033

Made in the USA
Middletown, DE
17 January 2019